# The Daniel Dilemma

# The Daniel Dilemma

STUDY GUIDE | SIX SESSIONS

## How to Stand Firm & Love Well in a Culture of Compromise

# Chris Hodges

*New York Times* Bestselling Author

NELSON
BOOKS

An Imprint of Thomas Nelson

*The Daniel Dilemma Study Guide*
© 2017 by Chris Hodges

Published in Nashville, Tennessee, by Nelson Books, an imprint of Thomas Nelson. Nelson Books and Thomas Nelson are registered trademarks of HarperCollins Christian Publishing, Inc.

Published in association with Yates & Yates, www.yates2.com.

All Scripture quotations, unless otherwise indicated, are taken from The Holy Bible, New International Version®, NIV®. Copyright © 1973, 1978, 1984, 2011 by Biblica, Inc.™ Used by permission. All rights reserved worldwide.

Scripture quotations marked NCV are from the New Century Version®. © 2005 by Thomas Nelson. Used by permission. All rights reserved.

Scripture quotations marked NLT are from the Holy Bible, New Living Translation. © 1996, 2004, 2007, 2013, 2015 by Tyndale House Foundation. Used by permission of Tyndale House Publishers, Inc., Carol Stream, Illinois 60188. All rights reserved.

Thomas Nelson titles may be purchased in bulk for educational, business, fundraising, or sales promotional use. For information, please e-mail SpecialMarkets@ThomasNelson.com.

ISBN 978-0-310-08857-8

First Printing August 2017 / Printed in the United States of America

Apr-16-2019

8277S2019O3_WB_C_16

# Contents

# Introduction

In the Bible, we read how a man named Daniel faced a dilemma. After the reigns of King David and his son Solomon, the nation of Israel splintered. Within a few generations, the ten northern tribes of Israel abandoned their faith in the living God and started worshiping idols. God sent warning after warning that disaster would strike if they did not turn back to him, but ultimately their disobedience led to the Assyrians conquering all ten tribes in 722 BC. The southern kingdom of Judah, where Daniel lived, also turned away from God. They were conquered by the Babylonians in 598 BC.

Daniel was taken into captivity with the other people of Judah. He was probably around sixteen years old when he was transported with thousands of other Jews to be slaves in Babylon. His situation was as bleak as it gets. There was no leader organizing a secret revolt, no legal recourse or government appeal to help him. On the surface, Daniel had no hope.

Yet Daniel never despaired or gave up. Over time as he served God faithfully, his character and conduct began to stand out to the Babylonians, because it was both respectful and resolute. Daniel didn't *conform* to the demands of the kings he served or the customs of the Babylonians, but he didn't act self-righteous, judgmental, or defensive either. His life journey wasn't always easy—he faced extreme difficulties, from watching friends endure a fiery furnace to being tossed in a lions' den. But in the face of dangerous circumstances and a foreign culture shifting around him, he never once wavered in his faith or dedication to God.

In response to Daniel's steadfast faith and commitment to truth, God demonstrated his supernatural power and honored the one who honored him by blessing Daniel with the respect of four different Babylonian emperors. These rulers included Cyrus, who granted the Jewish people freedom so they could return home. Talk about influence!

In this study, we will look not only at Daniel's example but also at Jesus' example of how we can stand up for God while still engaging and loving people in our culture. We will examine how we, like Daniel and Jesus, can become people of influence who stand out because of the way we relate to others, serve those in need with a willing spirit, and reflect the lovingkindness of a good God. We can be people who stand firm and love well.

Let's jump into *The Daniel Dilemma* to find out how.

# How to Use
# This Guide

## Group Size

*The Daniel Dilemma* video-based study is designed to be experienced in a group setting such as a Bible study, Sunday school class, or other small-group gathering. If the gathering is large, your leader may split everyone into smaller groups of five or six people to make sure everyone has enough time to participate in discussions.

## Materials Needed

Everyone in your group will need his or her your own copy of this study guide, which includes the opening questions you will discuss, notes for video segments, directions for activities and discussion questions, and personal studies in between sessions. You may also want a copy of *The Daniel Dilemma* book, which provides further insights into the material you are covering in this study. (See the note at the end of each week's personal study for specific chapters to read in the book to prepare for the next week's group meeting.)

## Facilitation

Your group will need to appoint a person to serve as a facilitator. This person will be responsible for starting the video and keeping track of time during discussions and activities. Facilitators may also read questions aloud and monitor discussions, prompting participants to respond and assuring that everyone has the opportunity to participate. If you have been chosen for this role, note there are additional instructions and resources in the back of this guide to help you lead your group members through the study.

## Personal Studies

During the week, you can maximize the impact of the course with the personal studies provided for each session. You can treat each personal study section like a devotional and use them in whatever way works best for your schedule. You could do one section each day for three days of the week, or complete them all in one sitting.

# In the World but Not of It

Truth without grace is mean. Grace without truth is meaningless.
Truth and grace together are good medicine.

CHRIS HODGES

# Getting Started

"Does it really matter what this movie is rated?"

"How should I vote on issues that contradict my beliefs?"

"When is it appropriate for me to bring up my faith with my coworkers of different faiths?"

Sound familiar? More and more Christians today are asking questions like these as they grapple with how to live out their faith in that world that seems to change at dizzying speed. We all feel the struggle between standing firm in our faith while loving others. Or, as Jesus described it, being in the world but not of it (see John 17:16).

It can be difficult to navigate. But as followers of Jesus, we have an important message to share. Jesus commanded us to go into the world and "make disciples of all nations" (Matthew 28:19), and his sacrifice on the cross makes it possible for *all* people—no matter how different they might seem from us—to find hope in a relationship with the living God. When those around us experience his forgiveness, they can begin living in the freedom of his grace.

The challenge, of course, occurs when our beliefs, convictions, practices, and lifestyles collide with those of the people we are trying to reach. God's Word instructs us to go one way, but they insist on going their own way. In such situations, we are faced with the responsibility to stand firm in our faith while continuing to love others like Jesus loves them.

Finding balance while living in this tension is what *The Daniel Dilemma* is all about. While the book focuses on the prophet Daniel's example of living faithfully within the secular culture of Babylon, in this study we will focus on the issues Daniel faced—issues we still face today—with Jesus as our model and guide. As challenging and frustrating as it may feel sometimes, there is a way to stand strong and love well.

So let's get started!

# First Impressions

For this first session, go around the group and introduce yourselves to one another, and then answer the following questions:

What one word would you choose to describe your feelings about starting this study? How does this word reflect your expectations?

How have you experienced the tension between loving others where they are in life and standing firm to God's principles in the Bible?

# Video Teaching

Play the video segment for session 1. As you watch, use the following outline to record any thoughts, questions, or points that stand out to you.

**Notes**

Being in the world but not of it

Jesus' prayer in the Garden of Gethsemane

Three things to help us navigate the tension:

> *Lord, sanctify me*

> *Lord, solidify me*

> *Lord, send me*

We're all called to make a difference

# Group Discussion

Take a few minutes with your group members to discuss what you just watched and explore these concepts in Scripture.

1. In the video, Chris shares about making changes in his life after becoming a Christian. What changes did you make after inviting Jesus into your life?

2. How did others, especially your family and friends, respond when they saw the changes you made after becoming a follower of Jesus?

3. Read John 17:13–19. What surprises you most about Jesus' prayer, considering that he was about to die the next day?

4. Why do you think Jesus asks God *not* to take his followers out of the world?

5. What comes to mind when you hear the word *sanctified* at the end of this passage? What does sanctified mean to you?

6. Jesus said, "You are the light of the world" (Matthew 5:14). What does it mean for you to let your light shine where others can see it?

# Individual Activity

Close out today's session by completing this short activity on your own.

1. Briefly review the video outline and any notes you took.

2. In the space below, write down the most significant point you took away from this session—from the teaching, activities, or discussions.

*What I want to remember from this session is . . .*

# Closing Prayer

Go around the room and share any personal prayer requests you'd like the group to pray about. Conclude your session by praying for these requests together. Ask God to work in each of your hearts throughout the week as you reflect on all you've covered during this first meeting.

## BETWEEN-SESSIONS PERSONAL STUDY

You're invited to begin reading Chris's exploration of Daniel as a model for how to stand strong and love well in *The Daniel Dilemma*. This week, read the introduction and, in preparation for session 2, read section 1, chapters 1–3, on "Culture's Greatest Impact—Confused Identities." The questions and exercises provided in this section are not intended to burden you with homework between group sessions but simply to help you receive the greatest benefit from reading the book and applying its principles to your own life. Write your responses and reflections here or in a journal or notebook dedicated to this study. There will be time for you to share your thoughts at the beginning of the next session.

## Reflection

In the video this week, Chris shared about the early struggles he experienced with his girlfriend and his buddies after he committed his life to Jesus. Although he was terrified of their responses, he discovered God had uniquely prepared the way for him to tell others about his faith. Spend a few minutes today reflecting on your faith journey since you first made the decision to accept God's gift of salvation in Jesus.

What have been the high points—times when you felt especially close to God and reflected this to others?

What have been the low points—times when you've drifted away from God or become swept up in worldly pursuits?

How have these highs and lows influenced your present ability to find the balance between standing firm and loving well?

. . . . . . . . . . . . . . . . . . . .

When culture shifts—and it always has and always will—
we tend toward the extremes, in part because they seem easier and
require less of us. We may feel so angry, threatened, and frustrated that
we want to withdraw from culture, attacking and condemning people who
don't agree with us. Or we may become so battle weary that we're tempted
to issue a blanket acceptance that avoids any cultural conflicts. But the
good news of the gospel means we don't have to become paralyzed by
extremes. We can be the calm in the midst of the cultural storm.

THE DANIEL DILEMMA, PAGES XVIII–XIX

. . . . . . . . . . . . . . . . . . . .

# Application

In the introduction, Chris cites the story of the woman caught in
adultery in John 8 as one of his favorite examples of Jesus balancing
truth and love. The religious leaders tried to trap Jesus into saying
something they could use against him, but he turned the tables on
them while still caring for the poor woman they had humiliated:

> As he was speaking, the teachers of religious law and the Pharisees
> brought a woman who had been caught in the act of adultery. They
> put her in front of the crowd.
>
> "Teacher," they said to Jesus, "this woman was caught in the
> act of adultery. The law of Moses says to stone her. What do you
> say?" . . .
>
> They kept demanding an answer, so he stood up again and
> said, "All right, but let the one who has never sinned throw the first
> stone!" Then he stooped down again and wrote in the dust.
>
> When the accusers heard this, they slipped away one by one,
> beginning with the oldest, until only Jesus was left in the middle of
> the crowd with the woman. Then Jesus stood up again and said to

*the woman, "Where are your accusers? Didn't even one of them condemn you?"*

*"No, Lord," she said.*

*And Jesus said, "Neither do I. Go and sin no more"* (John 8:7–11, NLT).

Who do you identify with most in this scene—the woman or the religious legalists? Why?

Chris explains, "[Jesus] doesn't condemn the woman like the religious legalists; instead, he shows her grace. But he doesn't let her off the hook either; he tells her to 'go and sin no more.' Jesus avoids the extremes of either-or by displaying both love *and* righteousness." Do you agree with Chris's explanation? Why or why not?

How have you faced a confrontational situation like this? What role did you play? Did you end up experiencing more grace or more judgment?

Thinking back over your life, when has someone demonstrated the same balance Jesus displays here, showing you both love and righteousness?

. . . . . . . . . . . . . . . . . . . . .

Knowing what we believe and why we believe it is foundational to our ability to be people of positive influence. Having God's truth as our point of reference not only allows us to withstand the swirling currents of cultural change, but it also allows us to extend a lifeline of grace to others around us.

THE DANIEL DILEMMA, PAGE 25

. . . . . . . . . . . . . . . . . . . . .

# Action

Finding spiritual balance involves engaging with the world without allowing it to pull you away from God. Would you describe yourself as someone who is currently too immersed in the world? Or someone who is too detached from the world? Explain your answer.

Engaging with the world in ways that demonstrate both strength and compassion requires constant reliance on God, his Word, and the Holy Spirit. Choose a place where you presently engage with the world around you on a regular basis. It might be your workplace, the local shopping mall, your school, your health club, or a city park. If possible, visit that place today and spend a few minutes walking through it and around it. Pray silently for God to use you there as someone like Daniel—a person who influenced those around him. Ask God to show you how you can demonstrate the love of Christ to others there.

Reflect on your experience after completing this exercise, and ask God to show you areas where you may be too engaged with the world and its influence. Ask him to search you and help you identify anything (shows, movies, websites, social media, music, places, people) that is pulling you away from your relationship with him. Take the necessary steps to remove these influences from your life.

---

This week, read the introduction and, in preparation for session 2, read part 1, "Culture's Greatest Impact" (chapters 1–3), in *The Daniel Dilemma*. Use the space below to note any key points or questions you want to share at the beginning of your next group meeting.

# Identity Theft

Our identities shift when we value those looking
at the art more than the Artist.

CHRIS HODGES

# Getting Started

Have you ever been whitewater rafting? Depending on the speed and depth of the river, you can experience anything from a comfortable float to high-intensity rapids. In fact, you will probably experience both of those in the same river, often going back and forth between the two without a lot of notice.

Engaging with culture often feels the same way. Even though we may have a lot of healthy confidence in our faith, each day we still end up in some rough waters, where today's culture tries to pull us away from whom God created us to be. Each time we make it through that section and into calmer waters, we know another rapid is just around the corner. That's the world we live in. There is constant tension between who God says we are and who the world says we should be.

This is why it's so important to dwell on the certainty of who God says you are and live out the purpose he made you for. In Jeremiah 1:5, God says, "Before I formed you in the womb I knew you, before you were born I set you apart; I appointed you as a prophet to the nations." Intertwined with who you are is God's unique purpose for your life.

Once you understand this purpose, you will know your true identity. While other people and cultural forces may attempt to define you, their false labels won't stick. Knowing who God made you to be keeps you anchored in his will and influences every decision you make and every risk you take.

*Purpose* is your identity in action, and when you're secure in that identity, your impact will make an eternal difference.

# First Impressions

Go around the group and answer the following questions:

What are some ways that our society tries to label people?

Looking back at your notes, what stood out to you in your between-session studies that you would like to share with the group?

# Video Teaching

Play the video for session 2. As you watch, use the following outline to record any thoughts, questions, or points that stand out to you.

**Notes**

The world tries to erode our God-given identity

Jesus' seven "I am" statements in the book of John

Two ways we find purpose in life:

*Go to the Source*

*Look at our design*

Four things we need to know about our purpose:

*I am a minister*

*I have a specific purpose*

*I have an opportune time*

*I can make an eternal difference*

# Group Discussion

Take a few minutes with your group members to discuss what you just watched and explore these concepts in Scripture.

1. In the video, Chris says our families, environments, and cultures often shape the way we see ourselves. How did these factors influence your view of yourself when you were growing up? After entering adulthood?

2. On a scale of 1 to 10, with 1 being "no clue" and 10 being "absolutely certain," where are you in your awareness of your God-given identity and purpose? Explain.

3. What person, event, or experience has helped you discover more of your true identity and purpose in life? Why did this catalyst have such a powerful impact on you?

4. Chris explained the four areas of God's identity for us: each of us is a *minister*, with a *specific purpose*, at an *opportune time*, to make an *eternal difference*. How do you see yourself as a minister with a specific purpose?

5. What are some of the opportunities God has given to you to make a difference for him?

6. A popular song some years back encouraged listeners to "live like you're dying." What does this mean to you? How would awareness of this affect your daily choices?

# Individual Activity

Close out today's session by completing this short activity on your own.

1. Take a few minutes to review the video outline and any notes you took.

2. In the space below, write down the most significant point you took away from today's teaching, activities, or discussions.

   *What I want to remember from this session is . . .*

# Closing Prayer

Take some time to go around the group and share any personal prayer requests, and then close this session by praying together as a group. In addition to praying over the group's requests, thank God for creating each of you uniquely and having a special purpose for every person in the room. Finish by asking him to strengthen your true identity and reinforce your divine purpose so you can shine your light in a dark world, just like Daniel did in Babylon.

Similar to what you did after session 1, the following questions and exercises are designed to help you apply this week's teaching and practice the personal application. As you deal with these powerful issues of identity and purpose, reflect on your responses and ask the Holy Spirit to guide you toward the next steps. You can write your responses and reflections in the space provided or in the journal or notebook you started last time. Once again, there will be time for you to share your observations and outcomes at the beginning of the next session.

## Reflection

In the video this week, Chris shared how his life could have taken different turns if he had not discovered his identity in Christ and begun to live accordingly. Imagine your life along similar lines. Think back on forks in the road where knowing God's truth about who you are and why you're here made a crucial difference. What might your life look like if you hadn't persevered to follow Jesus and obey God's Word?

How do you feel as you consider these possibilities?

How has God saved you from the false version of yourself you might have become?

. . . . . . . . . . . . . . . . . . .

You can also rest in the knowledge that within your unique identity, you have a very specific purpose. Not only did God create you to live in this particular season, but he gave you just the right personality, abilities, talents, and gifts to accomplish what you're called to do. You are not an accident. You are here on purpose for a purpose.

THE DANIEL DILEMMA, PAGE 16

. . . . . . . . . . . . . . . . . . .

# Application

As Chris mentioned in the teaching, Jesus made seven "I am" statements about himself, as recorded in the book of John. Read each of the verses in John listed below, and then write the metaphor Jesus uses to describe himself and the promise he gives to those who follow him.

| Verse(s) | Metaphor | Promise |
|---|---|---|
| 6:35 | I am the bread of life | Jesus will never leave me spiritually hungry— he fulfills both my physical and spiritual needs |
| 8:12 | | |
| 10:9 | | |
| 10:11 | | |
| 11:25–26 | | |
| 14:6 | | |
| 15:5 | | |

In addition to comparing himself to symbols like bread and light, Jesus also painted word pictures comparing foolish people with those who are wise:

> *Therefore everyone who hears these words of mine and puts them into practice is like a wise man who built his house on the rock. The rain came down, the streams rose, and the winds blew and beat against that house; yet it did not fall, because it had its foundation on the rock. But everyone who hears these words of mine and does not put them into practice is like a foolish man who built his house on sand. The rain came down, the streams rose, and the winds blew and beat against that house, and it fell with a great crash* (Matthew 7:24–27).

Why do you think Jesus says we must not only hear his words but also practice them?

Has there been a time in your life when you built your identity, purpose, and convictions on "sand," only to have it collapse? What was your "sand"—success, money, popularity, or something else?

Notice in the parable that the weather pattern was the same for the wise and foolish: "The rain came down, the streams rose, and the winds blew and beat against that house" (Matthew 7:25, 27). What does this parallel tell us about what to expect from the world?

What areas of your life are currently built on the rock of God's truth? Which areas feel a little shaky because of the sandstorm of cultural winds blowing around you?

What do you need to do to strengthen all areas of your life so you can withstand any cultural storm?

· · · · · · · · · · · · · · · · · · · · ·

If we want to maintain a worldview centered on Christ and live according to God's standards, then we must determine our core convictions. Just as a building must have load-bearing beams to support its structure, our worldview relies on beliefs determined by God's Word. Otherwise, when the culture-quakes of change occur, our worldview will collapse. Convictions require you to decide what's right ahead of time. They're not based on what feels good or seems right in the moment. They are, instead, the unmovable foundation upon which our lives are built.

THE DANIEL DILEMMA, PAGE 29

· · · · · · · · · · · · · · · · · · · · ·

# Action

Our core convictions often align with our identity and purpose. If we hold a false view of ourselves and struggle to live out of our God-given purpose, our beliefs may change when cultural trends shift. However, if we are sure of our true identity and purpose in Christ, we will be able to hold fast to what we believe regardless of cultural change. If you want to influence the world around you with the love of God, your belief in what God says is true must be your firm foundation. The enemy will find the places you might be more sympathetic to cultural ideas and try to move you away from your convictions toward false, though attractive, alternatives. The following questions are designed to help you identify some potential weaknesses and reinforce your convictions with God's Word.

Complete the following:

*Right now, the greatest cultural tension I'm facing is* _____
_____
_____
_____

*Usually, I handle this cultural tension by* _____
_____
*or by* _____
_____


*My concern about this cultural struggle is that it affects what I be-lieve about* _____
_____
_____


*Instead, I must remember what God says is true about this issue, which is* _____
_____
_____

_____

In preparation for session 3, read part 2, "Culture's Greatest Test" (chapters 4–6), in *The Daniel Dilemma*. Use the space below to note any key points or questions you want to share at the beginning of your next group meeting.

# You Are What You Worship

We are made to worship, and if we're not worshiping our Creator, then we're trying to put something else in his rightful place.

CHRIS HODGES

# Getting Started

It's easy to recognize what it is you worship. Just follow the trail of your time, your money, your attention, your loyalty, and your energy. Worship isn't about your religion, the church you attend, praying with your group, or singing praise songs; it's about what's going on in your heart. Simply put, worship is your response to what you value most.

God made you with a desire to worship, and if you're not worshiping him, you will find something else to put in his place. That's what *idolatry* is: offering your heart to false gods. Idolatry comes in many forms, not just in pagan statues and exotic shrines to false gods in the form of objects or animals. Culture bombards you every day with alluring idols of power, money, sex, and fame, each one asking you to bow before it.

If you're not anchored in Christ—if you haven't drawn a line in the sand that you refuse to cross—then your heart can easily become seduced by cultural gods and cave to temptation. The enemy can lead you astray and rob you of the purpose, peace, and joy that God created for you to experience.

But it doesn't have to be this way. You can refuse to cross that line. You don't have to attack those around you or become defensive, but you do need to remain attentive to what your heart is focused on. That way, you can stay strong no matter what you face. When you put God first in every area of your life, you can stand strong and love well—and influence the culture around you.

# First Impressions

Go around the group and answer the following questions:

What are some of the "idols" you see people worshiping in the world today—things they put first in their lives instead of God?

Looking back at your notes, what stood out to you in your between-session studies that you would like to share with the group?

# Video Teaching

Play the video for session 3. As you watch, use the following outline to record any thoughts, questions, or points that stand out to you.

**Notes**

Daniel's culture demanded he stop worshiping God

God wants to always be first

God is a jealous God

Order communicates priority:

*Put God first*

*Give him the first of everything*

*Expect him to bless the rest*

God blesses those who honor him

# Group Discussion

Take a few minutes with your group members to discuss what you just watched and explore these concepts in Scripture.

1. The Babylonians threatened Daniel's faith by trying to make him worship their idols and prohibit the way he worshiped God. Which of these two forces is most prevalent in your life right now? What has been your response?

2. Chris says, "order communicates priority." Do you agree with this observation? Why or why not?

3. Read Exodus 20:1–3. What do you think of when you hear the phrase "other gods"? What are the "gods of the people" around us today?

4. Read John 4:23. What do you think Jesus means when he says, "true worshipers"? What does it mean to worship God "in the Spirit and in truth"?

5. What impact does this kind of worship have on a person's relationship to the surrounding culture?

6. Chris says that when you put God first in all areas of your life, you can then expect God to bless the rest of those areas. Do you agree? Why or why not?

# Individual Activity

Close out today's session by completing this short activity on your own.

1. Take a few minutes to review the video outline and any notes you took.

2. In the space below, write down the most significant point you took away from today's teaching, activities, or discussions.

   *What I want to remember from this session is . . .*

# Closing Prayer

Go around the room and share any personal prayer requests you'd like the group to pray about. Once you pray over these requests, take a moment to thank God for one thing you're especially grateful for today. Then praise God for one of the reasons you love him, such as his power or his grace. Finish by praying that each person in the group would draw closer to God by spending more time with him in every area of his or her life.

As Chris shared in the video teaching this week, reflecting on what we worship can be troubling, especially when the way we live our lives doesn't line up with what we say is our priority. The questions and exercises in this between-sessions guide will help you identify areas in your life where you may want to reorder your time, your finances, or your focus to put God first.

# Reflection

As Chris shares in *The Daniel Dilemma*, worshiping God is a consistent choice, not merely an expression of how we're feeling when things are going well. Even when circumstances don't go the way we want, we still acknowledge God has a plan and continue to trust him. Worship keeps us grounded in what we can't see: the eternal kingdom of God advancing around us.

Although our culture continues to elevate individuality and promote people's rights to choose what's best for them, we know God is the source for how we are designed to live. The way He wants us to live our lives not only allows us to be closer to him but also makes a way for us to experience a full life of joy and purpose.

Today, spend a few minutes asking the Holy Spirit to help you look honestly at what you're worshiping that's getting in the way of your relationship with God. Then write your answers to the following questions:

What was your greatest takeaway from your group's last meeting? What continues to stand out to you about what you worship? What have you learned about your relationship with God this week?

On a scale of 1 to 10, with 1 being "never" and 10 being "all the time," rate the following statements:

_____ *I spend some time with God first thing when I wake up.*
_____ *I usually pay my tithe and offering before paying other bills.*
_____ *I'm glued to my phone, tablet, or computer.*
_____ *I listen to music that draws me closer to God.*
_____ *The shows and movies I watch reflect my core convictions.*
_____ *At work, I find time to pray silently or check in with God.*
_____ *The articles, blogs, and books I read strengthen my faith.*
_____ *I actively participate in my local church.*
_____ *I volunteer and serve those in my community.*
_____ *I read the Bible and think about what it means for my life.*

Based on your responses, which areas demonstrate your commitment to put God first?

Which areas are being influenced by culture and need attention?

. . . . . . . . . . . . . . . . . . . . .

Worship is respecting who God is and how he sees things.
It's acknowledging that he is God and we are his creation. The clarions of
culture want to force us to abandon our form of worship because they
find it offensive. Because our ongoing, faithful obedience to God and his
Word threatens those who want to undermine God's existence and his
role in our lives. And so our culture consistently and continually tries to
erode the truth about God and place his power in human hands.

THE DANIEL DILEMMA, PAGE 81

. . . . . . . . . . . . . . . . . . . . .

# Application

Several times in this video teaching, Chris referenced David's ability in Psalm 139 to give voice to our heart's desire to be closer to God. Using your favorite Bible translation, read through this psalm, and then answer the following questions.

In the first stanza (verses 1–6), David's words focus on God's in-depth knowledge of his children. How do you feel when you think about God knowing you in this same personal way?

That stanza concludes with the lines, "Such knowledge is too wonderful for me, too lofty for me to attain." What do you think David meant? Do you feel this same way?

How often do you praise God that you are "fearfully and wonderfully made" (verse 14)? How does this affect the way you see yourself?

How does this compare with the messages you receive from culture about your appearance, intelligence, and popularity?

David ends his song with the words, "Search me, God, and know my heart; test me and know my anxious thoughts. See if there is any offensive way in me, and lead me in the way everlasting" (verses 23–24). What "anxious thoughts" are you currently battling?

Is there anything in your heart that's keeping you from God? What do you need to tell him?

. . . . . . . . . . . . . . . . . . . . . . .

If we keep our hearts purely focused through continual prayer and praise and season our words with God's grace, then we don't have to worry about what others may think. God's truth has the power to set people free— this should fuel our desire to connect with others, not a smug attempt to prove we're right. We know some people won't want to hear what we have to say. Others may not like what we say, but they will respect us for speaking up and see our motive is not to be right but to be loving.

THE DANIEL DILEMMA, PAGE 88

. . . . . . . . . . . . . . . . . . . . . . .

# Action

If you want to influence the world and those around you with God's love, it is crucial to keep your focus on him. Perhaps the reason some Christians become defensive, spiteful, or self-righteous when interacting with others is because they have lost sight of their first love: their relationship with God. If we do not consistently worship God, it's easy to get caught up in proving others wrong and showing them we're right. The solution for this is to remain grounded in our relationship with God so we're motivated only by his love—a love that stands strong when necessary but also cares more about people than being right.

How often do you worry about what others think of you and your Christian faith? When was the last time it came up, directly or indirectly, while talking to someone who didn't share your faith?

How do you usually respond when a friend, coworker, or acquaintance comments on an important issue and expresses views different from your own?

Is there a more balanced, loving way to respond the next time this situation comes up? What can you say to show more of Jesus' love?

---

In preparation for session 4, read part 3, "Culture's Greatest Question" (chapters 7–9), in *The Daniel Dilemma*. Use the space below to note any key points or questions you want to share at the beginning of your next group meeting.

# Who's the Boss?

Pride is a "gateway" sin that offers an open doorway for our enemy
to drop in and tell us just how great we are and how we really
don't need God. It whispers, "Religion is just a crutch for
all those weak people! You're strong; you're better than that.
You're in control of your life." These lies embolden us to question
God and to start thinking he doesn't know what he's doing, to start
believing we know more than God knows.

CHRIS HODGES

# Getting Started

We live in a culture that's social-media obsessed and saturated with opinions, comments, likes, and retweets. We've become the center of our own little universes, convinced our opinions need to be heard regardless of the topic. We engage with a global audience, trying to be the ones who shout the loudest and longest to express ourselves because we're right and everyone else is wrong. And virtually everything around us reinforces the false notion that we can—and even should—control our own destinies.

But this social media obsession is simply a symptom of the cultural cancer plaguing our society: the sin of pride. In reality, it shouldn't matter to you what your friends on Facebook, your trusted news site, or your favorite celebrities think about today's hot-button issues. If you're committed to knowing, loving, and serving God, it shouldn't even matter what *you* think.

If you want to stand strong, love well, and make a positive difference in the lives of those around you, you need to focus on what God thinks. And he's given you his Word as a guide for knowing what he thinks. If God has already spoken about a topic or issue, then you and I don't need to form an opinion. We just need to keep pursuing the way, the truth, and the life that can be found only in Jesus.

This dedicated pursuit isn't easy. It requires you to lay down your agenda, humble yourself before the Lord, and trust he knows best. It requires you to lose your life in order to find it. It requires you to overcome pride.

# First Impressions

Go around the group and answer the following questions:

How would you define the word *pride*? How would you define the word *humility*?

Looking back at your notes, what stood out to you in your between-session studies that you would like to share with the group?

# Video Teaching

Play the video for session 4. As you watch, use the following outline to record any thoughts, questions, or points that stand out to you.

**Notes**

The problem with pride

What God is looking for in us

Jesus' example in the Garden of Gethsemane

Three attitudes toward lordship:

*I want what I want.*

*I want what God wants if . . .*

*I want what God wants—period.*

What happens when we follow Christ with humility

# Group Discussion

Take a few minutes with your group members to discuss what you just watched and explore these concepts in Scripture.

1. What do you think is the difference between *gratitude* ("I'm proud of how my kids are doing"), healthy *confidence* ("I take pride in my work"), and the kind of *pride* that's sinful ("My pride kept me from apologizing")?

2. Read Romans 12:1–2. What does it mean to offer yourself to God as a "living sacrifice"?

3. In the video, Chris describes three attitudes toward lordship ("I want what I want," "I want what God wants if . . .", and "I want what God wants—period"). Which describes how you relate to God right now?

4. Why is surrendering to God's way often challenging?

5. What are some ways culture encourages us to promote our-selves and think less of others? How do you handle these cul-tural influences?

6. Chris says pride is the "gateway" sin that often opens the door to other temptations and failures. Do you agree with him? Why or why not?

# Individual Activity

Close out today's session by completing this short activity on your own.

1. Take a few minutes to review the video outline and any notes you took.

2. In the space below, write down the most significant point you took away from today's teaching, activities, or discussions.

   *What I want to remember from this session is . . .*

# Closing Prayer

Go around the group and let each person share his or her personal prayer request, and then pray as a group to conclude the session. Tell God how much you need him, and ask him to help you be humble. Take some time to pray over the requests the group shared, making sure to focus on others' requests more than your own. Thank God for continually guiding you and demonstrating his faithfulness time and time again. End by thanking him for his goodness and mercy.

## BETWEEN-SESSIONS PERSONAL STUDY

As Chris shared in the video teaching this week, the sin of pride usually leads to either humility or humiliation. In Proverbs 16:18 we read, "Pride goes before destruction, a haughty spirit before a fall." We either learn to let go of our self-importance and give our desires to God, or we suffer the consequences and get what we think we wanted (even as we lose what matters most). The questions and exercises below are designed to help you apply the teaching and grow in humility.

## Reflection

How can you focus on "less of me and more of God"? The Bible tells us, "If [God's] people . . . humble themselves and pray," then he will hear us and forgive us (2 Chronicles 7:14). When you come before God in prayer, you begin to acknowledge your own limitations and God's infinite power. Prayer forces you to surrender to your Creator and trust his plan for your life. Consistently talking with God builds relationship and results in an even deeper, stronger trust in him. This kind of prayer communication grows into a constant lifeline—not just an "SOS" when things fall apart.

Spend a few moments today in prayer, asking the Holy Spirit to help you look honestly at areas of your life where pride is pulling you away from God. Then consider the following questions and write down your responses.

Is there an area of your life where you feel convicted to confess your pride? What is it?

Why is this particular area a fertile ground for pride? Is your pride masking fear, insecurity, or anxiety? Or is it just an area in which you simply want to be noticed and valued by others?

Think back on session 4 at the last group meeting. What stands out from your discussion? What continues to echo in your mind and heart? What might God be trying to tell you?

Are you more likely to brag and draw attention to yourself in a prideful way, or does pride manifest itself in more subtle ways (such as insecurity, anxiety, or false modesty)? Explain.

Review the following Scriptures related to pride and humility. Choose one verse to memorize as a way of grounding you in God's ways and not your own.

> When pride comes, then comes disgrace, but with humility comes wisdom (Proverbs 11:2).

> Pride goes before destruction, a haughty spirit before a fall (Proverbs 16:18).

> Pride brings a person low, but the lowly in spirit gain honor (Proverbs 29:23).

> Live in harmony with one another. Do not be proud, but be willing to associate with people of low position. Do not be conceited (Romans 12:16).

> Love is patient, love is kind. It does not envy, it does not boast, it is not proud (1 Corinthians 13:4).

> If anyone thinks they are something when they are not, they deceive themselves (Galatians 6:3).

*Do nothing out of selfish ambition or vain conceit. Rather, in humility value others above yourselves* (Philippians 2:3).

*But he gives us more grace. That is why Scripture says: "God opposes the proud but shows favor to the humble"* (James 4:6).

. . . . . . . . . . . . . . . . . . . . .

If we want to overcome pride in our lives, then we must turn from being self-sufficient back to being God-dependent. We must give him the credit for everything we have and acknowledge that we're just stewards of these many blessings. God doesn't bless us just so we can hoard a lot of money and buy stuff. He blesses us to be a blessing for others, to advance his kingdom, to reveal his love through the gift of salvation in Christ.

THE DANIEL DILEMMA, PAGE 114

. . . . . . . . . . . . . . . . . . . . .

# Application

During the video teaching this week, Chris referenced the story of the rich young ruler as an example of someone who was only willing to trust God conditionally. His response to Jesus' invitation falls in the category of responding, "I want what God wants if . . ." Take a look at what this young man's "if" might have been, and then answer the questions that follow.

*As Jesus started on his way, a man ran up to him and fell on his knees before him. "Good teacher," he asked, "what must I do to inherit eternal life?"*

*"Why do you call me good?" Jesus answered. "No one is good—except God alone. You know the commandments: 'You shall not murder, you shall not commit adultery, you shall not steal, you shall not give false testimony, you shall not defraud, honor your father and mother.'"*

*"Teacher," he declared, "all these I have kept since I was a boy."*

*Jesus looked at him and loved him. "One thing you lack," he said. "Go, sell everything you have and give to the poor, and you will have treasure in heaven. Then come, follow me."*

*At this the man's face fell. He went away sad, because he had great wealth* (Mark 10:17–22).

Why do you think Jesus responds at first by asking, "Why do you call me good?" What was Jesus forcing this man to confront?

It's striking that we're told, "Jesus looked at him and loved him" (Mark 10:21). Christ saw both the sincere desire in this man's heart as well as his passion for wealth—and still loved him. Why is it often difficult to see people clearly and still love them the way Jesus loved this young man?

What's the big "if" this young man used to make his obedience conditional? In other words, how would the rich young ruler have finished this sentence: "I want what God wants if _____"?

What conditions are you sometimes tempted to place on your obedience to God? What would it take for you to totally surrender and say, "I want what God wants—*period*"?

. . . . . . . . . . . . . . . . . . . .

We've all got to make some decisions about how connected to
the world we are going to be, how much we will allow it to sway us toward
what feels good or toward what God says. So how will you know what
should and shouldn't be in your life? You have a Holy Spirit who will convict
you. And you have a Bible that shows you the standard of God.
Between the two of them, you will know.

THE DANIEL DILEMMA, PAGE 139

. . . . . . . . . . . . . . . . . . . .

## Action

One way to practice humility is to serve others anonymously, showing them kindness and giving them a gift of your time, attention, or resources. Between now and the next session, do something for someone without that person knowing you did it. If possible, choose someone you can help that you might not normally choose to serve, such as someone with a different belief system or lifestyle. You could prepare a meal for the person, pay for his or her dinner at a restaurant, leave groceries on the persons' doorstep, or simply mail a note of encouragement. Let you and God be the only ones who know about this small act of service.

---

In preparation for session 5, read part 4, "Culture's Greatest Culprit" (chapters 10–12), in *The Daniel Dilemma*. Use the space below to note any key points or questions you want to share at the beginning of your next group meeting.

# Divided, Distracted, and Disturbed

When we realize that our days are numbered, then we realize the need to make them count. Only following God and living for him provides the kind of deep significance we crave and were created to enjoy.

CHRIS HODGES

# Getting Started

We all lead busy lives. We're busy at work, home, school, and church—running here and there, weighed down by errands, chores, projects, demands, responsibilities, and obligations. As a result, most of us find ourselves distracted by the next urgent demand. There's no time for rest, relaxation, or recharging our physical, emotional, and spiritual batteries.

However, God's Word reminds us of a sobering reality: our time here on earth is limited. The Bible tells us that "people are destined to die once, and after that to face judgment" (Hebrews 9:27). While we may not like this truth, remembering that our days are numbered can actually keep us focused on making the most of the time we do have.

Living with the reality of our mortality should motivate us to make better decisions. Any time we think we have more of something than we need, it's human nature to take it for granted. If there's plenty of food in our house, it's hard to remember to be thankful we aren't hungry. If there's plenty of money in our bank account, then we may not be wise about saving for the future.

But when we're down to our last crumb or last dollar . . . suddenly those things become precious. We no longer take them for granted. When we recognize our limitations, we're motivated to make the most of our life and the time we have left. We suddenly realize the only way to make a difference in the world is to make sure something different is going on in us—to make the most of each and every day.

# First Impressions

Go around the group and answer the following questions:

What does busyness look like in your life? What are some of the problems with maintaining an over-packed schedule?

Looking back at your notes, what stood out to you in the between-session studies that you would like to share with the group?

# Video Teaching

Play the video for session 5. As you watch, use the following outline to record any thoughts, questions, or points that stand out to you.

**Notes**

We need something to give

The four ways in which Jesus grew

The four ways we should grow

    *Mentally*

    *Physically*

*Relationally*

*Spiritually*

Everything flows out of our relationship with God

How we can love well and make a difference

# Group Discussion

Take a few minutes with your group members to discuss what you just watched and explore these concepts in Scripture.

1. Read Luke 10:38–42. Do you identify more with Mary or with Martha in this story? Why?

2. Martha was distracted by her preparations for Jesus' visit in her home. What are some things that often distract you from spending time with God?

3. In the video, Chris describes four areas we should concentrate on when it comes to using our time: wisdom, stature, relationships with others, and relationship with God (see Luke 2:52). What are you currently doing to grow in *wisdom*?

4. How can you be more intentional about resting and relaxing?

5. How many truly life-giving relationships do you have? What are some practical ways you can grow in these relationships?

6. What are some ways you experience God's presence? What can you do to spend more time with him?

# Individual Activity

Close out today's session by completing this short activity on your own.

1. Take a few minutes to review the video outline and any notes you took.

2. In the space below, write down the most significant point you took away from today's teaching, activities, or discussions.

   *What I want to remember from this session is . . .*

# Closing Prayer

Share any prayer requests you have on your heart with the group, and pray over these requests together. Also, ask the Lord to help you make the most of your time, and praise and thank him for how he provides rest and renewal in your life.

## BETWEEN-SESSIONS PERSONAL STUDY

Time is your most precious resource. It's the only thing you can't get more of, no matter what you do. So, as you take time to think through the following questions and exercises, engage fully with the purpose behind them: to know yourself better, to draw closer to God, and to influence those around you with the good news of the gospel. In other words, don't just complete this "between-sessions" study because you're supposed to or because you want to have something to contribute to your group's next meeting. Instead, pay attention to what your responses, and your feelings about them, reveal about your relationship with time—and your relationship with God.

## Reflection

As you've seen throughout these sessions, standing firm and loving well require examining your heart and resetting your soul's compass back to the "true north" of God and his Word. It's easy to get caught up in the hectic busyness of work, family, school, church, and community relationships and responsibilities. It's not that these duties and roles are bad; it's just that your time is limited and you need to focus on your top priorities, giving them your best hours, energy, and attention. Read through the following questions and consider what changes you need to make in order to realign your heart with God.

In *The Daniel Dilemma*, Chris provides four warning signs that can help you realize your life is out of balance and in the danger zone:

_____ *1. Sin seems more attractive than usual.*
_____ *2. Your emotions are inconsistent.*
_____ *3. You have become less productive.*
_____ *4. You can't hear God.*

How many of these describe you right now? Check the ones that apply. Has anyone close to you pointed them out or shown concern? What has been your response?

In Psalm 46:10, the Lord says, "Be still, and know that I am God." Stop and consider that for a moment. When was the last time you unplugged long enough to sit with God and listen to him speak? How often do you quiet your soul before him?

Spend a few minutes with God, praising and worshiping him and enjoying his presence.

. . . . . . . . . . . . . . . . . . . .

God's laws and principles are always for our protection, health, and well-being—not to limit us, inhibit our freedom, or force our obedience.

THE DANIEL DILEMMA, PAGE 190

. . . . . . . . . . . . . . . . . . . .

# Application

The Psalms are filled with reminders of our limited time on earth and how this awareness draws us back to God. Read through Psalm 103:13–18 below, reflect on its meaning, and then answer the questions that follow.

> *As a father has compassion on his children,*
> *so the LORD has compassion on those who fear him;*
> *for he knows how we are formed,*
> *he remembers that we are dust.*
> *The life of mortals is like grass,*
> *they flourish like a flower of the field;*
> *the wind blows over it and it is gone,*
> *and its place remembers it no more.*
> *But from everlasting to everlasting*
> *the LORD's love is with those who fear him,*
> *and his righteousness with their children's children—*
> *with those who keep his covenant*
> *and remember to obey his precepts.*

Describe how this psalm makes you feel. What jumps out or strikes a chord in your heart?

How might God be speaking to you through this? Is there anything you need to change about how you've been spending your time?

Make a list of the items and images that humans are compared to in this passage. In addition to these, what other comparisons or metaphors can you think of?

Based on this passage, what's the relationship between your obedience to God and the quality of your days on earth?

According to this psalm, what impact will your obedience have on future generations?

In a sentence or two, describe the impact you would like to have on the culture around you.

Next, write another couple of sentences on the legacy you want to leave with those behind you.

Now complete this sentence: "In order to influence culture positively and leave the legacy I want to leave, I need to spend more time

_____
_____

and less time _____

_____
_____."

. . . . . . . . . . . . . . . . . . . . . . .

Whether we're younger or older, we have to stop trying to do
what everyone else is doing. We have to quit saying yes to those who offer
us something that will take us in the wrong direction. Unless we set
boundaries and say no to nonessentials, we will never be able to make our
highest and best contributions to the things that matter most.

THE DANIEL DILEMMA, PAGE 182

. . . . . . . . . . . . . . . . . . . . . . .

# Action

If you want to become a person of influence like Daniel, you have to make tough decisions about how you spend your time. You probably spend time on too many things that don't need to be in your life right now. These may be well-intended or perhaps served a significant purpose in the past, but now they just pull you away from what matters most. If you're going to restore balance, find rest, and refocus on priorities, you must eliminate the nonessentials. Something needs to go!

In each of the following categories, write down at least one drain on your time and how it can be eliminated. This might be something you need to delegate at work so you're not always staying late, or it could be a social obligation that gives you nothing in return. Eliminate what's unnecessary—don't hold back!

**Area: Home**

Time Drains:

How to Eliminate:

**Area: Work**

Time Drains:

How to Eliminate:

**Area: School**

Time Drains:

How to Eliminate:

**Area: Neighborhood or Community**

Time Drains:

How to Eliminate:

**Area: Free Time**

Time Drains:

How to Eliminate:

Area: Other _____

Time Drains:

How to Eliminate:

_____

In preparation for session 6, read part 5, "Culture's Greatest Need" (chapters 13–15), in *The Daniel Dilemma*. Use the space below to note any key points or questions you want to share at the beginning of your next group meeting.

# What the World Needs Now

As followers of Jesus, we have real hope. And we're called to share it.
But how we share it makes a difference.

CHRIS HODGES

# Getting Started

During the seventy years of Daniel's captivity, he shared his faith with each king he served. Throughout four different leadership regimes, he gained influence and pointed others to God, all without compromising his beliefs. How did he do it?

It's simple. Daniel was *real*. His exceptional qualities and godly character attracted his captors and commanded their respect. He demonstrated what we must always remember in our interactions with others: *connect before you correct*.

Jesus' final command to his followers was to "go everywhere in the world, and tell the Good News to everyone" (Mark 16:15 NCV). Notice that Jesus didn't tell us to go everywhere in the world and try to convince people we're right or antagonize them into submission. Instead, he gave us the task—the *opportunity*—to help others know God the way we know him: as a generous and trustworthy Father who loves his children.

Sharing our faith is about relationship, not memorized answers or poised presentations. It's about being genuine, honest, and caring.

In Colossians 4:5–6, Paul says, "Be wise in the way you act toward outsiders; make the most of every opportunity. Let your conversation be always full of grace, seasoned with salt, so that you may know how to answer everyone." Paul doesn't say we have to have all the answers; just that our conversation should be full of grace and seasoned with salt. *Soaked in God's grace and salted for flavor*—that's the best recipe for sharing our faith!

# First Impressions

Go around the group and answer the following questions:

What do you think when you hear the phrase "share your faith"? Do you have a positive or negative reaction? Why?

What is the most valuable takeaway that you've had from this study as a whole? What have you learned, and how have you grown?

Looking back at your notes, what stood out to you in your between-session studies that you would like to share with the group?

# Video Teaching

Play the video for session 6. As you watch, use the following outline to record any thoughts, questions, or points that stand out to you.

**Notes**
The call of all Christians

An "evil eye" versus a "good eye"

Three ways we "see clearly":

*See ourselves clearly*

*See other people clearly*

*See eternity clearly*

How we make the ultimate difference to influence eternity

# Group Discussion

Take a few minutes with your group members to discuss what you just watched and explore these concepts in Scripture.

1. How often do you think about sharing Jesus with others around you? Daily? Weekly? Every now and then? Explain.

2. Read Matthew 6:19–24. What does it mean to "store up . . . treasures in heaven"? How can we do that in today's world?

3. What is Jesus' reasoning when he says we can't serve two masters? In your experience, has this proved to be true?

4. In the teaching this week, Chris shares about an encounter his family had with a waitress in a restaurant. When was the last time you sensed the Holy Spirit nudging you to say or do something for someone you didn't know well? How did you respond?

5. Is there anything you might do differently the next time you sense him prompting you? Explain.

6. What can you do to be a Daniel in the culture God has placed you? What can your group members do to continue to encourage you to stand strong and love well as you influence the world for Christ?

# Individual Activity

Close out today's session by completing this short activity on your own.

1. Take a few minutes to review the video outline and any notes you took.

2. Reflect on everything you've learned throughout the past six sessions. In the space below, write down the most significant point you took away from this study.

*What I want to remember the most from this study is . . .*

# Closing Prayer

Go around the room and share any personal prayer requests you'd like the group to pray about. Finish up by praying together for a couple of minutes, thanking God for all he has shown you, taught you, and given you throughout this small-group study. Ask for his continued blessing on each group member as you pray for one another's needs and requests.

## AFTER-SESSIONS
## PERSONAL STUDY

Congratulations! You've finished reading *The Daniel Dilemma* and completed the group study. This final set of questions and exercises is designed to help you take what you have learned and practice it in your daily life. If you've kept your responses and reflections in a separate journal or notebook, you will want to use it for your final review and assessment. If you've kept your answers in this guide, then you can flip back through the various "between-sessions" pages.

# Reflection

This entire study has been about finding balance so you can be more effective in how you influence others positively and make a difference in the culture around you. As you move forward, you will want to stay aware of the old tendencies or "default settings" you started with that needed changing. Review your past responses and reflections in the "between-sessions" personal studies along with the "Individual Activity" sections from sessions 1 through 6. After looking over them, answer the following questions.

What surprises you most as you review your responses and reflections? What has changed in you as you've gone through this study?

What do you expect your greatest struggle to be moving forward as you work to stand firm, love well, and make a difference? How can you use the examples of Daniel and Jesus to help you through that struggle?

How will you remind yourself to speak, act, and serve from a more balanced, eternally focused perspective when relating to people different than you?

Consider choosing a Bible verse to memorize or write down and carry with you that can serve as an ongoing reminder of how you want to influence the culture around you.

. . . . . . . . . . . . . . . . . . . . . . .

Everyone longs to be loved unconditionally. We all crave attention and appreciate it when others show interest in us and our lives. As Christians, we don't have to become everyone's best friend, but we should show the compassion, kindness, and honesty we see modeled by Jesus. He always put the relationship first. Jesus connected with people before he corrected them.

THE DANIEL DILEMMA, PAGE 209

. . . . . . . . . . . . . . . . . . . . . . .

# Application

In this week's video teaching, Chris mentioned the way Jesus related to the Samaritan woman at the well. Read through this encounter in John 4:4–13:

> *Now he [Jesus] had to go through Samaria. So he came to a town in Samaria called Sychar, near the plot of ground Jacob had given to his son Joseph. Jacob's well was there, and Jesus, tired as he was from the journey, sat down by the well. It was about noon.*
>
> *When a Samaritan woman came to draw water, Jesus said to her, "Will you give me a drink?" (His disciples had gone into the town to buy food.)*
>
> *The Samaritan woman said to him, "You are a Jew and I am a Samaritan woman. How can you ask me for a drink?" (For Jews do not associate with Samaritans.)*
>
> *Jesus answered her, "If you knew the gift of God and who it is that asks you for a drink, you would have asked him and he would have given you living water."*
>
> *"Sir," the woman said, "you have nothing to draw with and the well is deep. Where can you get this living water? Are you greater than our father Jacob, who gave us the well and drank from it himself, as did also his sons and his livestock?"*
>
> *Jesus answered, "Everyone who drinks this water will be thirsty again, but whoever drinks the water I give them will never thirst. Indeed, the water I give them will become in them a spring of water welling up to eternal life."*

In light of what you've learned participating in the study group, what stands out to you in this scene? Why?

This passage notes that Jews did not associate with Samaritans. Why do you think Jesus chose to ignore this cultural custom and surprise this woman by asking her for a drink?

Who are the people you encounter on a regular basis who might be considered "Samaritans" by cultural standards? How do you interact with them? How could you follow Jesus' example to connect with them in a more meaningful way?

Think about one way you can offer "living water" to those around you who seem spiritually thirsty. Make a plan so that you're ready to share some aspect of your faith the next time you sense someone's interest.

. . . . . . . . . . . . . . . . . . . . .

*When you're prepared and looking for them, you'll be surprised*
*how many opportunities will open before you. Remember: the goal is*
*to persuade, not coerce. And when we live a life that others find*
*appealing and authentic, it's easy to do.*

THE DANIEL DILEMMA, PAGE 212

. . . . . . . . . . . . . . . . . . . . .

# Action

As you've discovered, engaging with the world in ways that demonstrate strength and compassion requires constant reliance on God, his Word, and the Holy Spirit. Back in session 1, you were asked to visit a place where you regularly interact with others who may not know Jesus—your workplace, the mall, school, your gym, a local park or neighborhood. You were instructed to walk through this place and pray, asking God to use you as he used Daniel.

Now it's time to revisit the same place and spend some time praying again. While you're there, notice others around you, be sensitive to God's Spirit, and ask if there's someone you should approach for a friendly exchange or casual conversation. If so, listen to the other person and don't be too quick or aggressive about bringing up your faith or God's role in your life. Just listen. Ask the Holy Spirit to help you see and hear what this person is sharing with you. Look for opportunities that might arise to serve, help, or encourage this person. You don't have to tell him or her that you're doing it because you're a Christian; you can let the person figure that out by your attitude and actions.

If you don't feel led to interact with anyone, choose one person there and silently pray for him or her. You probably won't have any idea what's going on in that person's life, but God knows. Ask him to meet that person where he or she is and to satisfy that person's thirst for the living water that only Jesus can give.

After you've revisited this place, arrange to meet someone from your group and compare your experiences. Share what you enjoyed most about going back to this place, as well as what you struggled with or felt troubled by while you were there. Pray together and continue encouraging one another to be salt and light in the world around you. Celebrate the fact that you are making a difference for eternity!

# Leader's Guide

Thank you for agreeing to lead a small group through this study! What you have chosen to do is valuable and will make a great difference in the lives of others.

*The Daniel Dilemma* is a six-session study built around video content and small-group interaction. As the group leader, just think of yourself as the host of a dinner party. Your job is to take care of your guests by managing all the behind-the-scenes details so that when everyone arrives, they can just enjoy time together.

As the group leader, your role is not to answer all the questions or re-teach the content—the video, book, and study guide will do most of that work. Your job is to guide the experience and create an environment where people can process, question, and reflect—not receive more instruction.

Make sure everyone in the group gets a copy of the study guide. This will keep everyone on the same page and help the process run more smoothly. If some group members are unable to purchase the guide, arrange it so that people can share the resource with other group members. Giving everyone access to all the material will position this study to be as rewarding an experience as possible. Everyone should feel free to write in their study guides and bring them to group every week.

## Setting Up the Group

As the group leader, you'll want to create an environment that encourages sharing and learning. A church sanctuary or formal classroom may not be as ideal as a living room, because those locations can feel formal and less intimate. No matter what setting you choose, provide enough comfortable seating for everyone, and, if possible, arrange the seats in a semicircle so everyone can see the video easily. This will make transition between the video and group conversation more efficient and natural.

Also, try to get to the meeting site early so you can greet participants as they arrive. Simple refreshments create a welcoming atmosphere and can be a wonderful addition to a group study evening. Try to take food and pet allergies into account to make your guests as comfortable as possible. You may also want to consider offering childcare to couples with children who want to attend. Finally, be sure your media technology is working properly. Managing these details up front will make the rest of your group experience flow smoothly and provide a welcoming space in which to engage the content of *The Daniel Dilemma*.

## Starting Your Group Time

Once everyone has arrived, it's time to begin the group. Here are some simple tips to help make your group time healthy, enjoyable, and effective.

First, consider beginning the meeting with a short prayer, and remind the group members to put their phones on silent. This is a way to make sure you can all be present with one another and with God. Then, give each person one or two minutes to respond to the questions in the "First Impressions" section. You won't need much time in session 1, but beginning in session 2, people will likely need more time to share their insights from their personal studies. Usually, you won't answer the discussion questions yourself, but you should go first with the "First Impressions" question, answering briefly and with a reasonable amount of transparency.

At the end of session 1, invite the group members to complete the between-sessions personal studies for that week. Explain that you will be providing some time before the video teaching next week for anyone to share insights. Let them know sharing is optional, and it's no problem if they can't get to some of the between-sessions activities some weeks. It will still be beneficial for them to hear from the other participants and learn about what they discovered.

During the "First Impressions" section, help the members who completed the personal studies debrief their experiences. Debriefing something like this is a bit different from responding to questions based on the video, because the content comes from the participants' real lives. The basic experiences that you want the group to reflect on are:

- *What was the best part about this week's personal study?*
- *What was the hardest part?*
- *What did I learn about myself?*
- *What did I learn about God?*

There is a specific question written to help process each activity, but feel free to expand on this time or adapt the questions based on the dynamics of your group.

## Leading the Discussion Time

Now that the group is engaged, it's time to watch the video and respond with some directed small-group discussion. Encourage all the group members to participate in the discussion, but make sure they know they don't have to do so. As the discussion progresses, you may want to follow up with comments such as, "Tell me more about that," or, "Why did you answer that way?" This will allow the group participants to deepen their reflections and invite meaningful sharing in a nonthreatening way.

Note that you have been given multiple questions to use in each session, and you do not have to use them all or even follow them in order. Feel free to pick and choose questions based on either the needs of your group or how the conversation is flowing. Also, don't be afraid of silence. Offering a question and allowing up to thirty seconds of silence is okay. It allows people space to think about how they want to respond and also gives them time to do so.

As group leader, you are the boundary keeper for your group. Do not let anyone (yourself included) dominate the group time. Keep an eye out for group members who might be tempted to "attack" folks they disagree with or try to "fix" those having struggles. These kinds of behaviors can derail a group's momentum, so they need to be steered in a different direction. Model active listening and encourage everyone in your group to do the same. This will make your group time a safe space and create a positive community.

The group discussion time leads to a closing individual activity. During this time, encourage the participants to take just a few minutes to review what they've learned and write down one or two key takeaways. This will help them cement the big ideas in their minds as you close the session. Close your time together with prayer as a group.

Thank you again for taking the time to lead your group. You are making a difference in the lives of others and having an impact on the kingdom of God.